The Alien
and Other Plays

Compiled by Irene Yates

Contents

How to Read the Plays

The four plays in this book are for you to read aloud in small groups. There are six parts in each play, including the narrator. If your group is smaller than six, the narrator's part could be read by one of the characters.

Follow the play carefully and when it is your turn to speak, remember to say your part clearly. Try to speak the way your character would talk. If you think your character is loud and bossy then you should read the part in a loud bossy voice. If you are reading the part of a king or somebody very important, try to convey this in the way you read your lines.

1 Skim through the play and look over your parts.

2 Read your lines quietly to yourself.

3 Read the play aloud in your group.

4 Re-read the play and make sure that you use the right sort of voice for your character.

5 Swap roles and read the part of a different character.

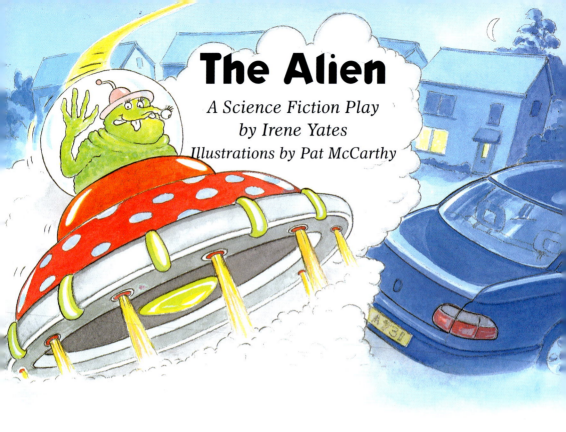

The Alien

A Science Fiction Play
by Irene Yates
Illustrations by Pat McCarthy

Cast

Narrator

Mum

Dad

Ben, aged 8

Tracey, aged 11

The Alien

The Alien

Narrator	*It is Saturday night and the Holly family are having their usual argument about what they are going to watch on the television.*
Ben	I want to watch *Night of the Aliens*.
Tracey	Well, you can't. Mum and I want to watch *Special Hospital*. So there.
Ben	Dad said I could choose this week.
Dad	Yes, I did. I remember telling him, last Saturday. We were all watching *Special Hospital* – just because you and Mum wanted to watch it – and I said Ben could choose this week.
Mum	That's only because you knew what he'd choose!
Tracey	Well, I don't want to watch a pointless science fiction film.
Ben	It's not a pointless film. It's really good. Everybody's seen it except us. It's got all these creatures from outer space in it –
Tracey	Creatures from outer space!
Mum	No such thing!

Dad   Come on – you don't know that...

Ben   ...and brilliant special effects...

Tracey   It's ridiculous – lots of actors running around in daft costumes...

Mum   Not as good as *Special Hospital*...

Ben   It's won film awards...

Dad   Okay. Okay. Tell you what. Let's toss for it. Heads we watch *Night of the Aliens*. Tails, it's *Special Hospital*.

Narrator   *Ben tosses a coin. It lands head up.*

Ben   Yeah!

Tracey   Oh no!

Mum   Never mind, love. We can always video our programme and watch it later.

Ben   You never know – you might enjoy it.

Narrator   *Tracey pulls a face at him. The family settle down on the sofa and switch on Night of the Aliens. To Mum and Tracey's surprise they get engrossed in it. They just get to the part when the alien goes into the house when there is a Bang! Bang! Bang! on their front door.*

Dad Who on earth can that be at this time of night? Someone go and see who it is.

Mum Well, it won't be for me. It's probably one of Ben's friends. You go, Ben.

Ben All my friends will be at home watching the film. It must be for Tracey. Tracey, you go.

Tracey It won't be for me. All my friends will be watching *Special Hospital*. I'm not going.

Narrator *There is another loud bang on the door.*

Dad I don't care who it is. Will one of you go and answer that door!

Narrator *Mum, Ben and Tracey all make for the door at once. They open it.*

Mum
Ben
Tracey *(Loudly)* AAAHHHH!!!

7

Tracey   *(Gasping)* Oh my goodness!

Narrator   *Standing in the doorway is a huge green alien.*

Alien   Gloddop!

Tracey   Help! What is it?

Mum   Dad! I think it's somebody for you! You'd better come here, quickly.

Ben   Quick Dad!

Narrator   *Dad comes to see what the noise is about.*

Dad   What's going on?

Narrator   *He sees the alien filling up the doorway.*

Dad   What … what … what's that?

Alien   Gloddop!

Mum   Well, don't just stand there! Are we going to ask it in or what?

Dad   Shut the door on it, quickly. Let it go somewhere else!

Narrator   *Mum, Ben and Tracey try to shut the door but the alien holds up its arms and the door disappears.*

Mum   Now look what it's done!

Alien   Gloddop!

Mum   I think we'd better let it come in.

Dad   Well, hurry up! Before the neighbours start to wonder what is going on. Bring it in.

Narrator   *They all walk backwards into the living room with the alien following them. They all sit down on the sofa. The alien squeezes in between Mum and Dad.*

Alien   Gloddop!

Tracey   How do we know if it's friendly?

Dad   We don't.

Ben   It looks friendly to me.

Mum   We could ask it.

9

Dad Go on then.

Narrator *Mum turns to the alien. She gives it a friendly smile and says…*

Mum Are you a friend?

Alien Gloddop! Gloddop!

Mum It doesn't understand me. Ben, you try.

Narrator *Ben gets up off the sofa and speaks to the alien in a robotic kind of voice.*

Ben I – Ben. I – friend. You?

Alien Gloddop!

Ben There, you see. It says its name is Gloddop.

Dad It says 'Gloddop' to everything. Tracey, you're good with animals and things. You try.

Narrator *Tracey gets up off the sofa and kneels in front of the alien. She puts her hands out to it and speaks in a sing-song kind of voice.*

Tracey Me, Tracey. Me like you. You like me?

Alien Gloddop! Gloddop! Gloddop!

Mum There! It *does* like our Tracey. It must be friendly.

Narrator *Mum puts her hand out to the alien, so that they can shake hands. She gives it her warm, comforting smile.*

Mum How do you do? We're very pleased to meet you. I'm Mrs Holly. These are my children, Ben and Tracey Holly. And this is my husband, Mr Holly.

Narrator *Dad stands up and puts out his hand. The alien takes it, holds it tightly and shakes it firmly up and down.*

Dad Well. It's very nice to meet you. I must say, we don't get many like you around these parts.

Narrator *The alien at last lets go of Dad's hand. Dad puts it behind his back, trying not to let everybody see him wince.*

Ben   *(In his robotic voice)* Can – you – tell – us – where – you – come – from?

Alien   Gloddop!

Tracey   That's nice. It comes from Gloddop.

Mum   Is that as far as Mars, or not?

Dad   It's probably further.

Ben   I wonder how it got here.
(To the alien) How – you – come – here?

Narrator   *The alien nods towards the window.*

Alien   Gloddop – gloddop.

Narrator   *Ben looks out of the window. There is a flying saucer on the road in front of their house.*

Ben   There's a flying saucer out there.

Narrator   *Mum takes a look.*

Mum   The neighbours won't like the alien parking there.

Dad   Well, we can't do anything about it. They'll just have to put up with it.

Tracey   I wonder how long it's staying.

Ben Ask it.

Tracey *(In her sing-song voice)* You stay here long? How long?

Alien Gloddop!

Mum Oh, that's all right then. It won't be here long enough to upset anybody.

Dad I suppose, when it's gone, I'll have to find the front door and put it back on.

Ben If you left the door off it would save us having to answer it all the time.

Dad That's true. Good idea.

Narrator *They all sit back down to carry on watching the television. In the film, the alien begins to pick out the humans, one by one, and exterminate them. The family feel a bit uncomfortable and they all begin to fidget.*

Mum   Perhaps it's time I made some sandwiches.

Narrator   *Mum turns to the alien.*

Mum   I bet you would like something to eat, wouldn't you?

Alien   Gloddop!

Mum   You see? It's probably starving. Poor thing! Ben, come and help me.

Ben   Do I have to?

Dad   Go on Ben. It's your turn.

Narrator   *Mum goes into the kitchen and Ben follows her, pulling a face. When they come back, Tracey and Dad have disappeared.*

Alien   Burp!

Mum   That's funny. Where have they got to? Ben, go out the front and see if they're messing with that flying saucer.

Narrator *Ben goes outside to look for Dad and Tracey. He can't see them anywhere. When he comes back, Mum has disappeared.*

Alien Burp!

Ben Oh. That's funny. Where's Mum gone?

Alien Gloddop!

Ben Oh, that's all right then.

Narrator *The alien pats the sofa for Ben to sit down. Ben picks up a sandwich and hands one to the alien.*

Ben Great! We can eat all the sandwiches ourselves now. *(In his robotic voice)* I – hope – you – like – cheese – and – pickle. *(In his ordinary voice)* My favourites.

Narrator *Ben munches the sandwiches. The alien moves closer and closer to Ben.*

15

Alien   Burp!

Narrator   *The alien gets up and goes out of the house. There is no sign of Ben.*

Alien   Gloddop, gloddop, gloddop, gloddop.

Narrator   *It just goes to climb into the flying saucer when it stops, thinks, looks around at the next door neighbour's house and burps again. Then the alien goes up the next door neighbour's path and bangs on the door, smiling to itself.*

What do you think will happen at the neighbour's house? Could this story really have happened?

Mice One, Kids!

A Modern Play by
Irene Yates
Illustrations by Rhian Nest James

Cast

Narrator

Mr Mills,
the headteacher

Dustman,
a helpful man

Kirandip, aged 9 – the
leader of the 'gang'

Jasbir, aged 8 –
a cheeky girl

Jack, aged 8 –
a friendly boy

Mice One, Kids!

Narrator *Kirandip and her friends, Jasbir and Jack, are in trouble as usual. They are standing outside the headteacher's room. Their headteacher, Mr Mills, is cross with them.*

Mr Mills How many times do I have to tell you? You're not supposed to be in the classroom at playtime. Why can't you do as you're told? You three are always in trouble. Let's see if you can keep out of trouble for the rest of the day. I do *not* want to see you outside my room again tomorrow morning!

Narrator	*The three children return to their classroom. They do their best to be good all day, but at home time …*
Jasbir	*(Proudly)* We've been good all day.
Kirandip	No one's told us off since playtime.
Jack	Must be a record for us! Come on, let's go home.
Jasbir	Let's not go straight home. I've got some money. Let's stop at the sweet shop.
Kirandip	Have you ever been round the back of those shops? My brother Ranjit said that some interesting stuff often gets thrown away.
Jasbir	What do you mean – interesting stuff?
Kirandip	Cardboard boxes and that bubble wrap that you can pop between your fingers. All sorts of stuff. Stuff that's been thrown away.
Jack	We're supposed to go straight home.
Kirandip	It wouldn't take long. We might find something *really* interesting.
Narrator	*They all look at each other. They know what they are supposed to do. But will they do it? Will they go straight home or go round the back of the shops?*

Jasbir
Jack   To the SHOPS!
Kirandip

Narrator *The three make their way down the side of the shops and into the yard at the back. There are huge dustbins and stacks of cardboard boxes.*

Jasbir It's just a load of rubbish.

Kirandip I can't see any bubble wrap.

Jack I wonder if there's some under all that cardboard?

Kirandip Once my brother Ranjit found a 50p piece in an old cardboard box.

Jasbir Great.

Kirandip Yeah, but our mum made him hand it in to the shop.

Jack We might find something even better.

Jasbir   What! In a load of old rubbish?

Jack   Well, it's worth looking. Anyway, this cardboard is really good stuff.

Kirandip   Yeah! If we had all this at school we could make a *hundred* models.

Jasbir   No, we couldn't – probably only about ninety nine. Anyway, are we allowed to just take this cardboard?

Jack   We could ask. It might not be very clean though.

Jasbir   But think how pleased Mr Mills would be with us.

Narrator   *They all look at each other. Would the headteacher really be pleased? With them?*

Jasbir
Kirandip   JOKE!
Jack

Narrator	*Suddenly they hear a noise coming from the pile of cardboard boxes. It's a faint kind of squeaking noise.*
Kirandip	Did you hear something?
Jasbir	Only your tummy rumbling!
Kirandip	No, no, I heard something. It came from those boxes. Listen.
Jack	Listen. *(Puts his hand to his ear)*
Narrator	*They hear the squeaks again.*
Kirandip	I heard it again!
Jasbir	So did I.
Jack	Listen!
Narrator	*The squeaking sound gets louder.*
Kirandip	It sounds like something is crying.
Jack	Maybe it's a little animal trapped in one of the boxes.
Jasbir	Sounds like more than one.
Kirandip	Yes. *Hundreds* of them – whatever they are.
Jasbir	We'd better have a look.

Jack   But whatever it is might bite us.

Kirandip   I'm going to have a look anyway. You can please yourselves.

Narrator   *Carefully, Kirandip tiptoes to the pile of rubbish where the squeaking is coming from. She tugs at a big sheet of cardboard. Then she gently lifts up one of the boxes.*

Kirandip   Wow!

Narrator	*The squeaking gets really loud and frantic.*
Jasbir Jack	What is it?
Kirandip	It's a little nest. *And* it's full of babies. I don't know what they are. They look like mice but they're not grey like mice usually are.
Narrator	*The others tiptoe over to have a look.*
Jasbir	Oh, they're so sweet! Look at their little twitchy noses! And look how long their tails are.
Jack	They're scared. You can see they're really frightened.
Narrator	*The little mice squeak even louder.*
Kirandip	Where's their mum? She must have gone looking for food. Let's keep really still and quiet – perhaps she'll come back.
Narrator	*They carefully cover the nest with the cardboard box.* *They stay very still.*

Kirandip Be quiet. Don't say anything at all.

Jack Don't *you* then.

Narrator *Suddenly they hear the noise of a dustbin lorry coming down the street. It bangs and clangs, stopping every now and then to collect rubbish.*

Kirandip Listen! It's the dustmen. They're coming to empty the bins!

Jack Oh no! They'll collect all this junk and take the nest with them! The babies will all be…

Jasbir *(Looking worried)* But they can't!

Kirandip Well, we'll stop them then.

Jack How are *we* going to stop them?

Kirandip We just will, that's all!

Narrator *The dustbin lorry comes to a stop at the front of the shops. The dustman comes round the back. The three stand, holding hands, in front of the pile of rubbish where the nest is.*

Dustman Come on, kids. Out of the way. I've got to shift all this rubbish.

Kirandip You can't.

Dustman What do you mean – can't?

Jasbir She means we … we … we …

Jack We want it for school.

Kirandip That's right. For making things.

Jack Models. Stuff like that.

Dustman You can't make models out of this. It's been out here for a week in all weathers – rain and everything. It's probably dirty.

Kirandip But we want it.

Dustman Sorry kids, but my job is to move it.

Narrator *The dustman starts pulling at the corners of the rubbish. It looks as if it's all going to crash down. The nest will crash with it.*

Kirandip Stop!

Jasbir You mustn't do that!

Jack You'll kill them!

Narrator *The dustman looks at them in astonishment.*

Dustman Kill what? Come on. What are you up to?

Kirandip We're not up to anything? But…

Jack There's a nest and we don't want you to take it away.

Kirandip It's no good. We'll have to show him.

Narrator *They pull the cardboard away to show the dustman the nest. The baby mice squeak wildly as soon as they're uncovered.*

Dustman *(Looking surprised)* Well, well, well! I'd say they are harvest mice, myself. Harvest mice – in the middle of a town!

Narrator *The dustman scratches his head.*

Dustman But how did harvest mice get here? I suppose they must have been carried in crates or boxes from a farm. The thing is, we'll have to protect them. Harvest mice are nearly all dying out, you know. Well done, you three, for finding them!

Narrator *The three children glow with pride. Suddenly they hear a little scampering. Everybody stands still.*

Jasbir It's the mother mouse!

Narrator *The mice make a huge squeaking noise to greet their mother.*

Kirandip I think they're pleased to see their mum!

Jack Let's make them all safe.

Narrator Carefully the children and the dustman put the cardboard back over the nest so that it's well covered. Then the three children get felt tip pens from their bags and make big posters saying, DO NOT TOUCH and CONSERVATION AREA.

Dustman Don't worry, kids. We'll get it sorted.

Narrator *Next morning at school, Kirandip, Jasbir and Jack are summoned to Mr Mills' office. What are they in trouble for now?*

Jack Going round the back of the shops, I suppose. It was all your fault, Kirandip! Someone must have seen us.

Kirandip And told on us.

Jasbir Yes, but if we hadn't gone that way we wouldn't have saved the mice, would we?

Jack And then they'd have gone in the bin. They would have all been killed.

Narrator *They gloomily knock on Mr Mills' door.*

Mr Mills Come in! Come in!

Narrator *The three children stand in front of him.*

Mr Mills   Now then, I had a telephone call last night – from the refuse collecting department.

Kirandip   We can explain…

Mr Mills   You were in a place where you shouldn't have been. Is that true?

Narrator   *They all blush, feeling guilty.*

Mr Mills   Hmmm. Well, you're coming into assembly with me now and I want you at the front.

Kirandip   To tell all the school how naughty we've been?

Narrator   *But to their surprise, Mr Mills smiles at them.*

Mr Mills   No. For once, you're not in trouble. You did exactly the right thing in saving the harvest mice. I'm very, very proud of you. And I want everybody to know it! And for once I can say 'Nice one, kids', or should I say 'Mice one, kids!'.

Narrator   *Kirandip, Jasbir and Jack all laugh.*

Do you think the children should have gone straight home after school? Why?

What do you think Mr Mills will say in assembly?

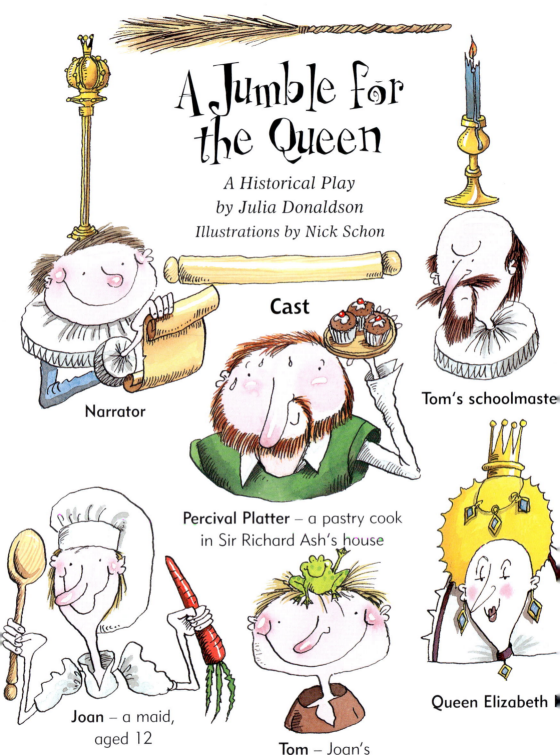

A Jumble for the Queen

A Historical Play
by Julia Donaldson
Illustrations by Nick Schon

Cast

Narrator

Percival Platter – a pastry cook in Sir Richard Ash's house

Joan – a maid, aged 12

Tom – Joan's schoolboy brother, aged 10

Tom's schoolmaster

Queen Elizabeth I

A Jumble for the Queen

Narrator   *Seven of the clock and a fine summer morning.*

Percival   *(Grumbling to himself)* Too fine! I'm sweating already. And I can't find the minced dates.

Narrator   *In Sir Richard Ash's house in Kent everyone is busy: the serving men and the stable lads, the butlers and the brewers, the carvers and the chambermaids…*

Percival   And the cooks!

Narrator   *How many cooks?*

Percival I'm too busy to count. But not enough pastry cooks. Joan! Joan! Where is that little lie-a-bed?

Joan I'm not lying in bed! I'm here and I'm cutting herbs.

Percival Cutting herbs! What about the custard tarts? Don't you know the Queen comes here tonight?

Joan Yes, Mr Platter. How could I not know? But the mistress said she needed some more herbs to strew on the floor. She said the Queen likes the smell of them.

Percival The Queen likes the taste of custard tarts, that's all I care about, and she won't be getting any at this rate. Now, run along to the dairy and fetch some more milk.

Joan Yes, Sir.

Percival Where did I put those minced dates? We'll never be ready in time!

Narrator *A quarter past seven of the clock. In a schoolroom ten miles away Joan's brother, Tom is late for school.*

Master Again! And where is your cap, Thomas?

Tom It…it blew away, Sir!

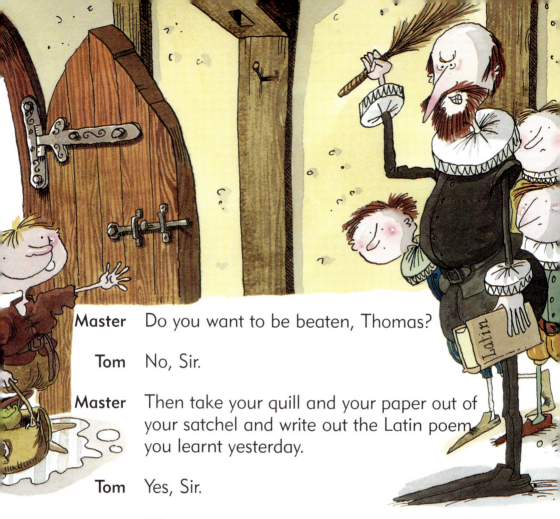

Master Do you want to be beaten, Thomas?

Tom No, Sir.

Master Then take your quill and your paper out of your satchel and write out the Latin poem you learnt yesterday.

Tom Yes, Sir.

Master What is that in your satchel, Thomas?

Tom Nothing, Sir.

Master Yes it is, it's your cap, and it's wet. Why is it wet, Thomas?

Tom I…I was catching frogs in it on the way to school, Sir.

Master I think perhaps you do want to be beaten after all, Thomas.

Narrator   *Ten of the clock. The Queen is leaving London. Not just the Queen: hundreds of people and thousands of horses: wagons full of clothes and jewels, pictures and ornaments, books, bedclothes…*

Queen   And beer – weak beer. Of all things, I detest strong beer.

Narrator   *The people of London throng the streets to watch the magnificent procession pass by.*

Everyone   *(Waving to the Queen)* Long live the Queen!

Queen   I thank you, good people of London. I am leaving you now for the fair county of Kent. But though I am away, may your love for me remain in your hearts till I return.

Everyone   God bless the Queen!

Narrator *Half past ten of the clock. In Sir Richard's kitchen the custard tarts are all made.*

Percival But not the quince pies! Joan! Joan! What are you doing with the vinegar? You should be peeling quinces.

Joan But the mistress asked me to make some tooth soap first.

Percival Tooth soap! Tooth soap! What do we want with tooth soap at a time like this?

Joan The mistress thought the Queen might need some for her teeth after eating all our puddings.

Percival She can't eat the puddings if we haven't finished making them!

Joan It won't be long, Sir. I've mixed the vinegar and white wine. I just need to add the honey and then boil it up.

Percival But what about the quince pies? We'll never be ready in time!

Narrator *Eleven of the clock. The schoolboys are having their dinner.*

Master Thomas, don't cut your nails at the table!

Tom I'm sorry, Sir.

Master What is the proper use of a penknife, Thomas?

Tom For shaping quills into pens, Sir.

Master And how do you say in Latin, 'The boy who cuts his nails with a penknife will be beaten'?

Tom Er … 'puer', that's … 'the boy'. 'Puer …' I don't know the rest, Sir.

Master And you didn't know your Latin poem this morning. Latin is the key to all knowledge, Thomas, haven't I told you that?

Tom Yes, you have, Sir.

Master I have told you in words, Thomas, but now I think that perhaps the birch rod will speak to you better than I can. You will bring me the rod after dinner, Thomas.

Tom Oh no, Sir. Please, Sir, no!

Master Oh yes, Thomas.

Narrator *Two of the clock. The Queen progresses towards Sir Richard's house. Crowds of cheering people line the roads.*

Queen And what bumpy roads they are! My poor horse stumbles and I am so jolted that I fear I shall not be able to sit down again for another week. Let us stop to greet the people.

Everyone *(Loudly)* Long live the Queen!

Queen I thank you, good people of Kent, for your love. Nothing can destroy this love of yours, not even time, which wears away rocks and mountains – and roads!

Everyone God save the Queen!

Queen Who is that boy I see running across the field towards us, as if for his life?

Narrator *The boy is Tom and he is running away from school.*

Queen See how he jumps over the gate in a single leap! Come here, my little leaper, I wish to speak with you.

Tom *(Bowing)* Your Majesty, I am your faithful servant!

Queen You are a scholar, I see, as well as a leaper. Pray open your satchel and show me what you are studying. What is this book?

Tom It's my Latin book, Your Majesty.

Queen But I see you have written a rhyme in English inside the cover.

Tom Yes, Your Majesty. I got into trouble for writing that. The Master said I should have been studying my Latin instead of scribbling.

Queen Read me your rhyme.

Tom 'The rose is red, the frogs are green, God bless Elizabeth, our noble Queen.'

Queen Are you sure you don't mean, 'The leaves are green'?

Tom It should be the leaves really, but I changed it. I like frogs. I got into trouble today for catching some in my cap.

Queen Well, Tom, you are not in trouble with me. I like frogs too. I have a little gold frog with an emerald back, who comes on my travels with me. I shall remember you and your verses! And now farewell, my leaping poet.

Narrator *Four of the clock. Someone is tapping at Sir Richard's kitchen door.*

Joan Tom, what are you doing here? Why aren't you at school?

Tom Stop asking questions and let me in!

Joan All right – in you come! But when Mr Platter comes back you'll have to hide.

Tom What's that you're making?

Joan Jumbles.

Tom *(Licking his lips)* Are they those thin crispy cakes? I love them! Can I really help?

Joan If you like, but wash your hands first. There's a pail in the corner. Now, tell me why you're not at school. Did the Master let you have a holiday?

Tom Not him! But I'm going to have a holiday – a long holiday. I'm never going back there again!

Joan Oh, Tom, you must go back!

Tom What, and get beaten black and blue? I hate it!

Joan Well, you can't stay here. Why don't you go home to mother and father?

Tom No, they'll just send me back to school. I'm running away to sea!

Joan No, don't do that – you'll get seasick.

Tom Well, I'd rather be seasick than go back to school. I shan't go back, I shan't, I shan't, I shan't!

Joan Oh, do stop thumping the dough like that! We're supposed to be making jumbles, remember?

Tom Why are yours all shaped like knots?

Joan They're not at all – look, these ones are shaped like rings.

Tom I've got a better idea. Look at this one!

Joan It looks like a frog!

Tom That's what it's supposed to be. And now I'll make an E shape to go on its back – E for Elizabeth.

Joan Why do you think the Queen would like a frog-shaped jumble?

Tom She likes frogs.

Joan How do you know?

Tom She told me. I've met her, you know.

43

Joan   *(With hands on hips)* Look, Tom, I haven't got time for any of your silly stories. If these jumbles aren't in the oven by the time Mr Platter comes back, I'll be in trouble.

Narrator   *Eight of the clock and a fine summer evening. Sir Richard's great chamber is full – and so are most of his guests.*

Master   Including me! That was certainly better than school dinners!

Narrator   *After the meal there will be dancing and fireworks. But first…*

Queen   I would like just one more of your delicious jumbles, Sir Richard. Why, here is one shaped like a frog! A frog with the letter E on his back. I have never seen the like before! Sir Richard, pray send for your pastry cook.

44

Narrator   *Sir Richard sends for Mr Platter who bows before the Queen.*

Queen   You have a skilful hand with the pastry, Mr Platter.

Percival   Thank you, Your Majesty, but I didn't make the jumbles – Joan did.

Queen   Then send for Joan.

Narrator   *Mr Platter sends for Joan who curtsies before the Queen.*

Queen   So this is Joan the jumble-maker!

Joan   I didn't make that one, Your Majesty!

Queen   Then who did?

Joan   Tom did.

Queen   Then send for Tom.

Joan   I'll fetch him, Your Majesty.

Percival Tom? Who is Tom? My head's going round.

Narrator *Joan fetches Tom who kneels before the Queen.*

Queen So it's the little leaper!

Master It's the little run-away!

Queen Is this true, Tom? Are you a run-away?

Tom Yes. I'm sorry, Your Majesty.

Master *(Angrily)* Sorry, are you? I'll make you sorry tomorrow, Thomas, you can count on that.

Queen Do I understand Tom, that you are not your Master's favourite pupil?

Master Your Majesty, the boy is always late, he loses his cap, he jumbles his Latin, he…

Queen Pray silence! We are not in school now. Tom's Latin may be a jumble, but his jumbles are fit for a Queen. I have a pastry cook who could do with an apprentice like you. Would you like the job, Tom?

Tom (*Enthusiastically*) Yes, Your Majesty!

Queen Then the deal is done. But now it is time to dance and make merry. Do you like dancing, Joan?

Joan I love it, Your Majesty.

Queen Then we shall see if you can leap like your brother. Sir Richard, lead us to your gallery, and we shall dance the night away.

Narrator *The music plays, the fireworks fly,*
Drowning out the watchman's cry:
'Twelve o'clock,
Look well to your lock,
Your fire and your light,
And so goodnight.'

What did Joan have to prepare for the Queen's visit?
Describe Tom's school life.

Real Dragons Roar

A Fantasy Play
by Jacquie Buttriss and Ann Callander
Illustrations by Carla Daly

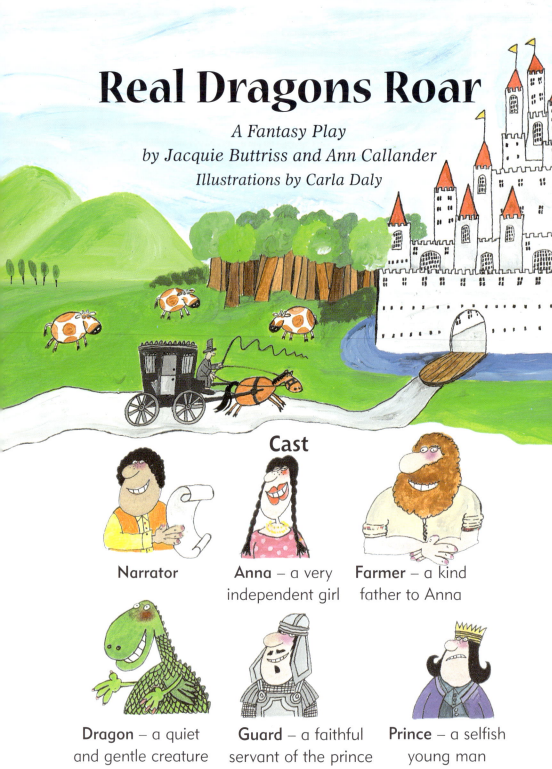

Cast

Narrator

Anna – a very independent girl

Farmer – a kind father to Anna

Dragon – a quiet and gentle creature

Guard – a faithful servant of the prince

Prince – a selfish young man

Real Dragons Roar

Narrator *Long ago, in a far away kingdom, there lived a dragon. But he wasn't an ordinary dragon. He was a very friendly dragon. He didn't breathe fire when strangers walked past his cave.*

Dragon I don't even smoke.

Narrator *He wore a pair of brightly coloured socks which he pulled right up to his scaly knees.*

Dragon I don't want my sharp claws to hurt anybody.

Narrator *And he never roared.*

Dragon *(Covering his ears)* I hate loud noises.

Narrator *The dragon liked a quiet life. Best of all he liked reading books and eating fudge.*

Dragon Especially both at once!

Narrator   *The dragon had many friends but his best friends were a farmer and his clever daughter, Anna.*

Dragon   She makes really good fudge.

Narrator   *Now, in the same kingdom, there was a very selfish prince who lived in a castle.*

Prince   I don't see why I should have to share things with anyone. After all, I am a prince. The trouble is I'm bored. No one will play with me.

Guard   I'll play a game with you, your highness.

Prince   Oh, all right. Go and get the snakes and ladders.

Narrator   *The guard went away and the prince stared out of the castle window.*

Prince   *(Looking fed up)* It's hopeless playing games with the guard. He gets everything wrong.

Narrator   *Just then, the guard came back carrying a small ladder.*

Guard   I couldn't find any snakes but I've found this ladder, your highness.

Prince   Oh no! Not that kind of ladder. I want the game of snakes and ladders.

Guard   I'm sorry, your highness. I'll go and look again.

Prince   No, don't bother. We'll play hide and seek instead.

Guard   Yes, your highness. I like hide and seek.

Prince   I'll go and hide, because I know all the best places. You count to 100.

Guard   But I can only count to 29, your highness.

Prince   Well, count to 29 very slowly.

Narrator   *The guard began counting very slowly, while the prince ran off to hide.*

Guard   18…19…20…29…coming!

Narrator *Meanwhile, the farmer and his daughter were planning to visit the dragon.*

Farmer Let's take the dragon some books to read and a basket of food.

Anna I've made him some fudge too.

Narrator *So they set off to visit their friend, the dragon, but when they got to his cave, they found the dragon looking miserable.*

Farmer *(Looking concerned)* What's the matter?

Anna Aren't you well? I've brought you some fudge.

Dragon Thank you.

Narrator *The dragon gave a big sigh and popped a piece of fudge in his mouth.*

Farmer Tell us why you are so sad.

Dragon It was that book.

Farmer What book?

Dragon The one you gave me about St George.

Anna Didn't you like it? I thought you might like to read about another dragon.

Dragon Yes. But St George rescued a maiden in distress and killed the dragon.

Farmer Oh, don't worry. Nobody kills dragons nowadays.

Anna Especially friendly dragons like you.

Dragon Why is it always the knight who rescues the maiden in distress? Why can't a dragon rescue a maiden?

Farmer I'm sure you could, but there aren't many maidens in distress around any more.

Anna Thank goodness!

Dragon But I want to do something exciting, and be famous. I want to be a hero.

Narrator *He popped another piece of fudge in his mouth and a big tear rolled slowly down his scaly cheek.*

Anna Don't worry, Dragon. I'll go and pick some flowers to cheer you up.

Narrator *Meanwhile, back at the castle, the prince was bored. The guard came back.*

Prince What's the good of playing hide and seek if you don't come looking for me?

Guard Oh, I forgot I was looking for you and I went off to hide.

Prince You're no good at hide and seek. Oh, what can I do now?

Guard We could play another game.

Prince But you get them all wrong. No, I've got a better idea. Let's go for a ride and we can look for someone who is good at playing games.

Guard Yes, your highness.

Prince Go and tell the groom to saddle two horses.

Guard   At once, your highness.

Narrator   *The prince and the guard rode towards the village. They saw Anna picking some flowers.*

Prince   *(Pointing to Anna)* There's a girl over there. Perhaps she knows how to play games. Quick, go and talk to her.

Guard   What shall I say?

Prince   …um, you could ask her what time it is.

Guard   But we already know what time it is. My tummy's rumbling. It's tea time.

Prince   Never mind. I'll speak to her myself.

Narrator   *The prince rode up to Anna.*

Prince   Can you help us?

Anna   What is the matter?

Prince   My guard and I are looking for someone.

Anna   Who?

Prince   Someone who can play games better than anyone else in the kingdom.

Anna   What kind of games?

Prince   Well, I am particularly good at chess. Do you know anyone who plays chess?

Anna   Yes, me! I like playing chess.

Prince   Then I challenge you to a match at the castle.

Anna   All right. But I must tell my father first.

Prince   No. It's getting late. We must go now.

Anna   But… but…

Prince   Guard. Seize this girl. Bring her back to the castle.

Guard   Yes, your highness.

Anna *(Loudly)* Let me go. Help!

Narrator *Inside the cottage, Anna's father heard Anna shouting. He rushed outside.*

Farmer Hey! What's happening? What are you doing with my daughter? Where are you taking her?

Narrator *The prince and the guard did not answer. They were already riding away towards the castle with Anna.*

Farmer Oh, what shall I do?

57

Narrator *The farmer thought hard and decided to go and see his friend, the dragon. The dragon was sitting in his cave darning his spare socks.*

Farmer You must help Anna. The prince and the guard have taken her away to the castle.

Dragon That's dreadful. But what can I do?

Farmer You can rescue her.

Dragon Who, me?

Farmer Yes. You are the only one who can help her.

Dragon You mean she's a maiden in distress?

Farmer Yes.

Narrator *The dragon was delighted. Here was his big chance to be a hero.*

Dragon But… how?

Farmer Here, I've brought a book about dragons. Perhaps that will give us some good ideas.

Dragon I hope so!

Narrator *They looked at the dragon book together and read about all the things that a dragon can do.*

Farmer   It says here that you can terrify people with your sharp claws.

Dragon   Can I really? I'd better take off my socks and see what I can do. *(Takes off his socks)*

Farmer   My goodness! Your claws are frightening!

Dragon   What else can I do?

Farmer   You can roar so loudly that people will run and hide.

Narrator   *The dragon opened his mouth and gave a great roar. The farmer was so frightened he ran to hide behind a tree.*

Dragon   Come back here! I'm just starting to enjoy myself. What else does it say in the book?

Farmer   It says here that you can breathe flames.

Narrator   *The dragon took a deep breath and blew such enormous flames that they burnt the grass outside his cave. He was so surprised that he nearly fell over!*

Dragon   Wow! I didn't know I could do that!

Farmer   Well done. You never know what you can do until you try.

Dragon   That's what my teacher used to tell me at dragon school. But I never believed her!

Farmer   Come on then. Now we must go and rescue Anna.

Dragon   I think I'd better have a piece of fudge first.

Narrator   *The dragon and the farmer set off together for the castle. They walked up to the huge castle door.*

Farmer   How shall we get through this thick wooden door?

Dragon   Don't worry. I'll burn it down. Just watch!

Narrator   *The dragon blew with all his might and the door disappeared in a burst of flames.*

Farmer   Well done!

Narrator   *Then the guard began to shoot arrows at the dragon. But the dragon roared so loudly…*

Dragon   ROAR!

Narrator   *…that the guard ran away to hide.*

Guard   *(Running away)* Help!

Farmer   Look. Here comes the prince with a huge silver sword.

Prince   You might frighten the guard, but you don't frighten me!

Narrator   *The dragon's knees trembled.*

Dragon   I think I'd better have another piece of fudge. *(Pops a piece in his mouth)*

Narrator   *Then the dragon remembered he was a fierce dragon and he showed his sharp claws and he roared loudly…*

Dragon   R-O-A-R!

Prince   You d-d-d-don't frighten me.

Narrator   *Then he blew fiery flames at the prince. The prince's coat caught fire.*

Prince   *(loudly)* Help! Help!

Narrator   *The guard heard the prince's cries and ran over to the well. He filled a bucket of water and threw it over the prince.*

Prince   Thank you, Guard. What a clever thing to do. You've saved my life.

Narrator *Meanwhile, the dragon and the farmer rushed into the castle to look for Anna. She was sitting in a velvet chair and looking down at a chess board.*

Farmer Anna!

Anna Shhhh! I'm trying to concentrate.

Dragon Anna! I've come to save you.

Anna Oh, Dragon. Don't be so old-fashioned. Can't you see I can look after myself?

Dragon But I roared a terrible roar and showed my sharp claws and I blew fiery flames at the prince.

Anna I wondered what all the noise was about. But now be sensible and put your socks back on. The prince and I are in the middle of a game of chess.

Storyteller   *From that day on, the prince and Anna became very good friends. The prince forgot all about being selfish and he started to be kind instead.*

Dragon   The guard and I are very good friends too.

Guard   Yes, and the dragon always shares his fudge with me.

Narrator   *So, Anna, the prince, the dragon, the guard and the farmer all lived happily ever after.*

Anna   If you believe that you'll believe anything.

How does this story differ from other traditional stories?